MW01274563

PEACE OF MIND

IN THE MIDST OF THE STORMS

LYNITA REGIS

Life Chronicles Publishing
Give your life a voice!
ISBN: 978-1-950649-41-9

Editor: Melissa Caudle
Cover Design: Life Chronicles Publishing
Life Chronicles Publishing Copyright © 2020
lifechroniclespublishing.com

All rights reserved. No part of this book may be reproduced in any form or by any electronic or mechanical means, including information storage and retrieval systems, with or without permission from the publisher or author, except in the case of a review, whereas quotes of a brief passage embodied in critical articles or in a review.

TABLE OF CONTENTS

INTRODUCTION

This book is a compilation of short stories and poems about enduring life's heartbreaking storms. My experiences have led me to find peace, even though it would seem impossible. My hope is that everyone who reads these short stories and poems will find the peace you deserve and need.

Lynita

1

MY MOMMA'S HOUSE

My first memory recall was…

It was a sunny day, and I was standing on the front porch of our new home. I was there with my mom; she was short with beautiful milk chocolate skin, and always well-spoken. That day my mother was so excited, yet calm. It was as if I could feel her energy fluctuating. This day was very special for her because we were getting a new home. At the time, I did not understand how big of a deal it was to buy one.

The house was a huge two-family home with an upstairs kitchen, a basement, and an attic. I had seven siblings, five sisters and two brothers; our grandmother also lived with us. My mother decided to move the kitchen downstairs and to make extra bedrooms for all of us to live comfortably.

I remember the tavern next to the parking lot located on the corner of our house and there was a single-family brick home on the other side of our house. It seemed like a pretty nice neighborhood.

Once we moved into the home, my mother was very happy, and she would sing songs with me like, *Little Red Caboose*. We would play and wrestle all the time, but she would always win. When my mother played with me, I felt like it was her way of displaying love to me.

The house had a nice size backyard, and my grandmother planted a garden once we settled into the home. There was plastic over the furniture for guests in the front room to make sure that it stayed free from any stains, and it also protected it. My cousins would come to visit on the weekends all the time I enjoyed them very much.

We had a nice size front porch, so we would just hang out, and family and friends would come to visit in the summer. One evening we were playing double-dutch on the sidewalk while the grown folk sat on the porch. I instructed my cousin not to let anyone interrupt us, but she did anyway. She made me so mad that for the first time, something inside of me said, "Hit her with the rope," so I did, and then I ran and hid until they left our home to go back to Illinois.

Then something changed, and things were never the same again. Instead, there was always something going on in our home. Once the fighting and the cursing started, it seemed to never end. I don't exactly remember what the fighting was all about, but I know that it caused me much pain. The energy in my house was so negative that I cried and plugged my ears most of the time. My mom was busy tending to my special needs sister, so there wasn't much attention for me. Someone would always take us to the park or a play area so we wouldn't be exposed to the drama that was going down. I do not recall who took us.

I was told that the house was haunted by a ghost named the Old Lady and I was taken to the park to be removed from being further traumatized by the ghost. I believe now that it was Jesus who made a way to escape mentally for me.

2

I LIKE SUMMERS
ON HAMILTON STREET

During this time in my life, my brothers would make homemade go-carts from wood and use the bike's handlebar for the steering wheel. We would ride these go-carts during the summer in our neighborhood on the sidewalks. It was so much fun, but we always had to be home before the streetlights came on.

One evening I was being pushed on the go-cart and ran right into a tree in front of the house; it knocked me out. They told me later that I stopped breathing and I still have a scar today from that accident. I always enjoyed spending time with my siblings. During this time, my oldest brother would teach my niece, nephew, and me how to fight. We learned many techniques and we would try them out on each other to prepare ourselves for whenever the time came to defend ourselves. Later in life, fighting taught me valuable lessons. I became a protector and survivor.

We would often go to the beach because it was within walking distance to the house. My family would go to the beach, but sometimes it would be just some of my siblings because I was too young to go by myself. We would run and play with a beach ball and enjoy being by the water. I love being in the water; it is very calming for me, even though I cannot swim. As I think back, I know why I love the water so much. It was peaceful, and I loved the warmth of the sun beating on my skin.

POEM

The Porch

*The front porch was a place we really enjoyed
summer and spring.*

*As the car went by one after the other, some
would blow and wave.*

*It was fun with go carts, hopscotch and marbles,
So innocent yet naïve to what life was really
about,
Playing dodge ball, jumping rope and kickball
brought a smile to our faces.*

*Reflection is so important for healing to begin,
To be the best you can be.*

3

THE STRUGGLE,
MY STEPDAD AND HIM

We had a trusted friend of the family whom everyone seem to like that would come over and visit us; he was about five years older than I was. He was a close friend of my brothers. Sometimes he would play with us. One day he was playing with all the children, swinging us around, but he would rub my body against his when it was my turn. I don't know if he did it to anyone else. Other times he would do things like touch my body or even dry hump me. I never told anyone about what he was doing.

One day, I told him that I needed some money, and he gave me some change. I gave the change to one of my family members friend to buy me some peanuts from the corner tavern. My mother often bought us chips and peanuts from there, and I was hungry.

I was too afraid to tell anyone what he was doing because I thought my family would hurt him badly. I did not want him to get in trouble; I said to myself that *after all, I did ask for money, and my clothes always stayed on*. I was not afraid of him, but I was afraid of what would happen to him. I remember, as a little girl hearing my mother say, "If you are going to be disrespected or be taken advantage of by a man, then, you had better get something from dealing with that man. Hearing my mother say that, I knew I needed to get something every time this guy touched me. That's why I asked him for some money. I did not see anyone carry on like this, but I knew what I was supposed to do in my mind. I acted on the words I heard my mother say instinctively.

The abuse didn't stop there. After that happened, someone who lived across the street from us, and one of their sons touched me on several different occasions in the same manner. I didn't think anything of it at the time. I believe that it was something that I was beginning to think was normal. I wasn't shocked or afraid and I didn't understand at a young age why this was happening. That was the last time I ever experienced sexual abuse in my home.

After that experience, I remember things getting hard for us at home; the memory brings me a cold, dark feeling. My mother began to struggle financially, and there were times we barely had enough food to eat. Sometimes the electricity was turned off. Even as a child, I could sense that my mother was sad, and I felt bad for her. All the stress affected me in many ways, but I did my best to bury my feelings.

My oldest brother taught me how to be tough and not cry. He told me it was a sign of weakness if I cried. So, whenever I needed to express my hurts, pain, and emotions, I would find somewhere to hide (and even to this day, I cry in silence most of the time, afraid to be vulnerable to anyone).

Stepdad

I remember my stepdad coming home from being on the road and parking his semi-truck in front of the house. There was a tree in the front of the house, and his truck would break some branches off because the top of the truck was tall. He was not at the house much. I believe that played a role in the bad behavior of some of my siblings.

I heard that he started relationships with other women. My stepdad was a long-distance truck driver, so my mom and stepdad were separated most of that time.

My mom met a man who would help her out from time to time while my stepdad was away. He seemed to love her, and he supported her financially. During this time, I think she was doing what she had to do to take care of us children with little help from anyone else. I never saw him at our house, but he would park around the corner. However, he would stop coming over when my stepdad came home from being on the road. Whenever he came back home from driving, it was a very exciting time for us, everything would return to normal, and life was good. He would fill the refrigerator and cabinets up, and my mother was happy again. He would sit and play with us, and things would be normal again.

POEM

The Power of the Tongue

*Silence is golden- is applied whenever
wisdom is not present.*

*To be quiet is necessary to
avoid speaking before thinking.*

*Take the time to consider the power
of the tongue, be slow to speak.*

*Once the words come out,
they cannot be retrieved.*

*Many pains can be voided by
considering the impact words have
upon others.*

Peace of Mind

4

DEAR SISTER

This was an already tough time for all of us being separated by the state, and then tragedy struck again. All of our lives were changed forever with the news of my sister's death. My sister was one of the oldest of eleven children when the state took us, and we lived in foster care.

My mother came to pick us up for the service. It was so hard to go to the funeral and see everybody crying and screaming. The room was full of so much pain. I will never forget my cousin falling out and people standing at the casket for what seemed to be a long period. This was the first time I ever attended a funeral; I was only seven years old. Afterward, we went to my sister's house to eat with family and friends, and then my mother took us back to the foster home. But it was different going back this time; it felt strange like I no longer belonged there anymore.

I realized that I would never see my sister again; no more visits, hugs, or treats. I wouldn't get to see her face ever again; no more sounds of laughter or seeing that beautiful smile of hers. I felt horrible inside; just the thought of her made me cry and put my heart in a place of sorrow. The one person who treated me special and was very protective of me was now gone.

I remember one time, we were all in the kitchen of our old house sitting in the front of the oven trying to stay warm, and an argument broke out. I ran outside to get away from the situation.

When I tried to come back into the house, the door was locked. My sister came to open the door for me and asked me who put me out in the cold. I was so scared to tell her the truth that I lied and blamed it on my brother so that I would not get into trouble. She went off on him; I quietly left the kitchen. Her death brought about so much sorrow and pain that would affect me for generations to come.

We would finally get to come back home, and that is when I started to be the primary caregiver for my special needs sister once we got back home.

I would clean up after her and keep the bedding clean also while dressing and bathing her. Once back with our mother, after telling the caseworker that I did not want to live with her, she called me out in the living room and asked me why did I respond to the caseworker in that manner. I did not say it to hurt her; I was a kid speaking my truth, but it changed our relationship forever.

Through all of the moving around, the verbal abuse never stopped toward me. My mom was upset with me ever since the caseworker asked me if I wanted to go back home with my mother, and I did not want to go back home and live with her anymore.

She would call me black, ugly, and bald-headed regularly and never apologized for the verbal abuse that I endured. At the time, I just wanted to go to my mom's only on weekends because the foster-care home was quiet. She felt as if I betrayed her when she was doing her best to get us back. So, once we were returned to her care, it changed our relationship forever. I was just in the second grade at the time. She was drinking all the time because I believe she was depressed. But through all that she said to me,

"I'm still protective of you girls when it comes to men."

POEM

Foster Care

*Life has taken me through changes;
this much is true.*

*Some of them good, but most of them
bad.*

*I miss my family, late at night when
all eyes are closed shut,*

*I smother face in the pillow as I weep,
not making a sound,*

*Quiet as a mouse to not alert anyone
around.*

I tell myself everything will be okay,

*Praying to God to be back with my
Mom one day.*

5

EYES CLOSED YET OPEN

The first day of school, my mother put my hair into braids called platts. I did not like them at all. But it did not matter to her, so off to school I went. Once I got settled in again, we would move constantly. I was so tired of being the new kid at school all the time. It became embarrassing to me, and I rarely made friends because I knew it wouldn't last long, anyway.

I did not want to go to school, but I knew, at least, I could have lunch. Even though sometimes getting lunch would be a hit or miss because she did not turn in the paperwork, and I would not get a hot lunch. This went on for most of my childhood.

Sometimes we went hungry, but whenever we had pork steaks, corn, and rice, that meant life was good during that time. My mother was afraid to get food stamps because she thought it would put us in the position to be taken away again and put back into the system. Some days my mother would make a meal out of flour and lard, yes flapjacks and gravy, and we were glad to have that instead of nothing. She would have credit at the corner store, but when that reached the limit we couldn't get any more food.

Looking back now, I understand that it was her fear of losing us that kept us hungry. I think it was because my disabled sister went into the foster care system twice, and once she got her back, she did everything in her power to keep her, even if that meant us going hungry at times. As a child, I did not understand why she conducted herself in that manner.

Then my oldest sister sent her kids to live with us. I think it was for a summer, and we were all very close. I loved having my nieces and nephews at the house with us; even my sisters' son who passed away would come to visit. He lived with his father's side of the family, they were nice people, and they loved him. Yet he would still come over to our house, even if we did not have electricity for the lights, heat, or food.

It seemed to help my mother, somewhat, when my nieces and nephews came to visit because I think she wanted to be a good grandmother to them. We began to become stable, and I was happy about that. My mom tried to slow down on her drinking; I know she was really trying to keep it together.

One thing my mother did was sing Christian songs, and I would sing along with her and her friends, even when she would drink. One of my mother's friends had several dogs, and her house smelled just like her dogs. I really did not like going with her to visit that lady's house. The smell was so strong whenever we left, we would also smell like her dogs. But she was a good friend to my mother; we even moved in with her for a short while. She let us move into her house on the top floor, and it was separated by the kitchen. No matter how hungry I was, I never ate anything from her house.

We continued to move around eviction after eviction. I knew my mother was doing the best she could, but it was just hard to be doing it alone. I felt bad for my mom.

I look back now, and I know it was even worst for her then I thought it was. After losing four children and having a stroke, all that trauma had taken a toll on her.

During these times, my niece, and nephews and I would be all over the place like the little rascals. We would walk across town on the railroad tracks, hang out in the ravine, and go to the apple orchards. One day we were hungry, so we walked across town to my brother's house, and when we got there, he was gone. So, we went into his room where he had his own kitchen and living area, but he shared the bathroom with others. We began looking for food, but we only found onions, seasoning, flour, and grease, so we decided to fry some onion rings. My niece and I were in the kitchen, and then I walked into the living room area. My nephew had been smoking a cigarette and threw into a pile of clothes. It started a fire. I panicked because the fire was next to a TV, and I thought that it might blow-up or explode.

I started telling them to get out of the building to make sure they were all safe. However, we decided to try to put the fire out ourselves. We threw some flour on the fire and smothered it. All that was left was a little smoke.

We heard a knock on the door; it was my nephew's father. He asked us why we were there, and we told him that we were looking for something to eat. He gave his son a spanking and went to the corner store and brought us back something to eat. We started to get creative when trying to find something to eat; we would go to the apple orchards and the park to eat pears from a tree and several other fruits. In Wisconsin, we grew peaches, plums, pears, cherries, and rhubarbs; something was better nothing. We would go to a neighborhood center called, Break-Through and eat free lunch five days a week during the summer.

POEM

The King

*Lost in the forest, blinded
by being too close,*

*Vision can make things blurry without
the right prescription.*

*Be willing to accept your diagnosis
while learning to adjust,*

*Then be grateful and humble for the
clarity.*

*It is such a sense of freedom when you
know your end game is Heaven,*

*Touchdown what a win, time to do that
dance of praise and worship as you
join the only King - Jesus!*

6

HOLDING ON
BY A STRING

My oldest sister moved one state away, and this made our lives better when my mother would visit her. We would move back and forth for years to come until one day we all lived in the same house. My family lived on the top floor, and my sister had the first floor.

I was in the seventh grade at the time, and I had been in the same school for two years; life was good! I made some friends and had my first crush; his name was Sean. He had freckles and dark brown hair. I thought he was so cool, like Fonzie from *Happy Days,* and he knew how to wear a pair of jeans. Needless to say, he paid me no attention at all.

Then there was a Hispanic kid a little older than me; he was fine from head to toe! So, I made friends with his sister to get closer to him, but he started dating another girl, and I did not like her at all.

I started hanging out with some other kids around the neighborhood. My mother told me to be inside before the porch light came on, but I would sneak right back out my bedroom window as soon as I could. One evening, I was trying to climb back into my bedroom window, and I almost fell because we lived on the second floor. I would use my neighbor's stairwell to get in and out, then one evening, my mother, was standing there, and I almost fell to the ground. From that day forward, I had to keep my door open, so that was that.

Shortly afterward, another one of my so-called friends had a boyfriend, and she wanted me to go with her to his house. When we got there, he had another friend there that I had no idea about. His friend told me to sniff something, it was liquid in a small brown bottle. I pretended to inhale, but the fumes alone had a strong effect on me. I quickly told them that I had to go check-in, and I would be right back. Once I got home, I slept until the next day. I never spoke to her again.

The following day I went to the store with my niece, and I would be the look-out for her to keep the clerk busy while she stole big block candy bars. We had the nerve to get an empty plastic bag from the same store. Once back at the house, my mother overheard us talking about stealing the candy and we got in big trouble. My sister gave us both a spanking and took our candy. She gave the candy to the other kids in the house. I felt bitter about the way she treated us. I started yelling, "Double jeopardy!" We were being punished two times for the same offense.

That didn't stop me from getting what I wanted. The next day in class I was caught chewing gum, and it made me upset because I thought that the teacher was trying to embarrass me in front of the whole class. The next morning I left home earlier and stopped by the store to supply the whole class with Hubba Bubba watermelon flavored gum. While inside the store, I put several packs of gum into my pocket and was standing at the counter to purchase the rest of the packs with the few dollars I had in my pocket. The cashier asked me to empty my pockets, and I did, they asked me what my name was, and I referenced to being a boy, so I replied, "Marvin Butler," in a deep voice. They let me leave with the gum that I had the money to pay for. I was told to never steal in their store again, or I would no longer be allowed in there. After leaving the store, I headed to school and shared the gum I did have with the whole classroom.

The school was a long walking distance from my house, and one time I met a girl, and we became friends. I would go to her house and play all the time; we would play board games and play with her dolls; she had a lot of dolls. My friend lived two blocks from my house, and her family were gypsies. They moved around a lot. Her mom was nice, but I didn't talk to her much. She told me she would be moving away soon, which made me sad, and I even cried. She said I could go with them if I wanted. I seriously thought about it, but something deep inside me told me no, so I did not go.

Then one day I came home, and my house was completely empty. I was scared as I sat on the front porch. It was getting dark, and I wanted to cry, but I was afraid someone would see me or hear me. I put my hands up to my face to muffle the sounds that I wanted to scream, I was in distress and my palms were sweaty. I got myself together and walked to the payphone to call my aunt collect. Back then, we didn't have cell phones, and you either had to drop coins into the payphone or ask the receiver to pay for it. Soon, she pulled up to get me in my unclc's clean, shiny red car and took me to my sister's house. That is when I found out where my family was located. The city had condemned our house, and they forced us to move out. I was at school at the time it happened, so when I finally got home, everyone was gone. I was totally relieved to know that everyone was okay.

My experience of living with my sister still came with many challenges. We lived in the Mary Jane projects for low-income families; living there changed my life forever. My sister kept a clean home, and the worst part of living with her was chicken noodles at the end of the month. I lived with my sister off and on for years because my mother could not keep stable housing. None of us had ever lived in the projects before.

By this time, I was in the eighth grade and had to catch several buses to go to school every day. I barely had clothing to wear and bus fare, but I hung in there.

POEM

Back and Forth

To and fro we would go,

not knowing the time or the place.

Destinations sometimes a blur,
doing her best yet lack so much,

not having too many people to whom
she could trust.

Off again, not knowing the next move
that was to be made,

just holding on sometimes by a string,

hoping that we would soon find a place
to rest.

7

THE WATERFRONT

My mother finally found a place for us near the waterfront, in the city where I was going to school. At one time, this was the place to live, but that was such a long time ago. The neighborhood was rundown, now. I made friends with some rough girls who lived at these apartments, but they were cool with me. My mother didn't know I was taking money out of her purse, and even when she would hide it, I would still find it and get whatever I wanted.

I used the money to take my new friends shopping, and one evening we went to a high school game, and we all had on pink matching outfits. We were having a good time until this boy yelled out and asked if I was a boy wearing pink. The girls stood up for me, but I was so embarrassed I took off running for what seemed to be forever. Finally, I stopped running, only to realize I was lost in the dark. Fear swept over me, and I was confused as to which way to go.

I began to cry and pray, then cry and pray some more. I had no sense of direction. I was afraid of headlights coming down the street, and all those things my mother said to me started to overwhelm my mind. Things like, *somebody will snatch you out there in the dark, so come home before the streetlights come on or bad things happen under the cover of darkness.* I realized that no one was coming to get me, so I kept on praying, and after walking for a while in different directions, I made it home. I was never so happy to see this place in my life.

After getting into the house, I saw a rat! I had never seen a rat before, and it was frightening for me. I grabbed two chairs and went into my grandmother's room to tell her about my experience of getting lost in the dark. I then proceeded to tell her that I would be sleeping on the chairs every night from that day forward. With a calm voice, my grandmother said, "Please do not sleep like that; instead, come sleep in my bed."

In my mind, I felt like the rat could climb the legs of the chair. I really did not want to sleep in any bed, but I climbed into her bed, anyways. Her bed sat pretty high because she had one box spring and two mattresses. So, I snuggled under the heavy homemade quilts, very close to her.

There in the bed, she put her palm up to cup my face, and I was soon sound asleep. My grandmother was an amazing person. I will never forget how she trusted me and loved me; she was always honest, kind, and gentle. Often, she would send me to the store to get her W. E. Garrett snuff and she would put it inside her bottom lip and had an empty can to spit in. My grandmother was a woman of her word.

I will never forget when I started my menstrual cycle, I stood in the bathroom one day after school and I thought I was dying. I was never told to expect this, so I was totally freaked out. I trusted my grandmother. Scared out of my mind, I went to her crying, screaming that I was dying. She showed me so much love. She told me to sit down and let me know that I would not die and that this was natural for every young lady.

Even though we were close, it brought me even closer to her. After that, we talked about everything under the sun.

As memories flood my mind… I will never forget the news of my grandmother's passing. We were all asleep when my sister's boyfriend delivered the news by yelling out, "Grandma is dead!!!" I heard it but did not want to believe it. Grief instantly overwhelmed me, and I jumped up and tried to run out of the house. All I wanted to do was die by running in front of a semi-truck. But they would not let me get out of the house; I eventually calmed down because I thought suicide was wrong. It hit me hard, but I had to go on with life and heal.

After my grandmother's passing, I just didn't feel like going to school at all. One day I stayed in bed and slept the whole day. The next thing I remembered, a week had gone by, and I was still unable to pull myself together to make it back to school. I guess the stress of moving so much and the loss of my grandmother had taken a toll on me, and I felt helpless. I tried homeschooling because of all the constant moving from one city to the next but it took its toll, and it didn't seem to work either.

POEM

No Direction

*There I was running and had
no sense of direction.*

Crying out to God to direct my path.

I knew in my heart it would be alright.

*There in the dark, no street lights
insight.*

*My heart pumping so fast, I felt so
overwhelmed.*

This was unknown territory for me;

*I had to stay calm, so the mind could
see.*

*Focus, I repeated to myself over and
over again,*

*Trying not to go in circles back to
where I had begun.*

Peace of Mind

*I see some lights ahead, feeling of
relief,*

*Now back in my neighborhood,
rather than on my street.*

8

MOVING AGAIN

We moved again, and this time, we stayed with this man who was good to us; however, he was old enough to be my grandfather. He wore overalls, name brand old-school loafers, and he didn't drive. Instead, he rode a bike with a basket in the front to get around town. He was a good friend to my mother and helped her out financially. She was getting the help that she needed from him to keep us off the streets and ensure that the state would never take her children again. She feared losing us to the system so, she would rarely get any welfare from the state, and that made it harder for her to support us as children.

While living with the old man, we had our own space; he also had a sofa sleeper. Many times, Sharon (my special needs sister) and I would sleep in the living room. I guess so our mother could see us. She had her ways, and I believe that she had trust issues with men to some degree. I can't say that I blame her, giving my past abuse. Mom would date or hang out with guys old enough to be my grandfather, maybe she thought it was safe having young girls around older men. We were taught not to be in grown men's faces or sit on their laps. Even though she had her issues, she was very protective of us.

My brother came over one day and put a jerry curl in our mother's hair. It was beautiful, and her hair was down her back. It made her feel good; it was much better than the wigs that she would wear. Then my brother said he would do my hair.

I started to make friends while living there, and we started hanging out, so I invited them over to watch my transformation. Three of my friends lined up on the couch, waiting to see what my hair was going to look like. I was so excited, yet anxious. Then as everyone watched him take my hair from each of the rollers one by one, my hair just flopped because it did not take. I was disappointed and embarrassed, and he felt bad for me as well. So, I went back to combing my hair straight back again. Living here was cool. I met some new friends and tried to enjoy them and the comfort of being stable.

Some children in the neighborhood were considered to be the "bad kids." They would walk by the house, laugh, and point fingers at me, saying that my mom's friend was a crazy old man. They called him crazy because the kids would step on his grass to steal apples from his tree in the backyard, so he shot his gun in the air several times to scare them off.

One day, some boys I knew in the neighborhood had a club in a garage and invited my best friend and I to hang out with them. Once inside, there were clouds of smoke, and it was thick. They had huge weed joints. At first, I thought to myself, *why would they want to give us weed for free*? Then, I started to feel a buzz; I told them that I had to check-in, and I'd come right back.

Once I got home, my other brother was there, and he told me to make a phone call for him. At the time, we had a rotary telephone. I made several attempts to make a call but could not get it right. He then asked me why my eyes were red. Let me tell you, my heart dropped because he knew what was going on, but I lied and blamed it on eyeliner make-up, not thinking I smelled like weed. But I'm sure he knew all along.

One evening, I went into the house and headed to the kitchen where the old man was sitting in a chair. He seemed confused and babbling. I could not make out what he was trying to say to me. I know that he did not drink, so I yelled out for my mother. He wound up in the hospital and later passed away. He was a very nice man.

The day after he died, his so-called family awakened us. We had never seen or heard from any of them, we knew only one of his dear friends. Once inside, they just started rumbling threw his belongings, opening dressers with no regard to our presence at all. They were disrespectful and rude. They made us leave, and we could only take what we could carry away on foot because my mother did not drive. Back to the projects to live with my sister, again.

My mother was drinking and tired one night, and she had a disagreement with my sister and fell at the step leading into the house. When I woke up the next morning and went downstairs, to my surprise, my mother was sitting in the middle of the floor where she was the night before. It was alarming because she was an early bird my whole life. She would be up before 6:00 a.m., like clockwork, and it was past 9:00 a.m. I knew that something was wrong, so I called 911, and when they arrived, she had a broken hip. I will never forget her screaming while they tried to get her through the narrow doorway.

At the hospital, she suffered a stroke, and it paralyzed her entire upper right side, which was her dominant side. Once she got back home, she did not do any physical therapy at all. There were times when she would get out of the house, and I would go looking for her. One time, it was snowing, and I tried to follow her footsteps, which led me to a neighborhood friend of the family, and she was just sitting there enjoying their company with no care in the world. I was so relieved that she was safe and in good hands.

One evening I was walking with a friend in the rain, and this guy yelled out to us. I thought for sure he was trying to get her attention, but to both of our surprise, he was talking to me. He turned out to be a very nice gentleman with no drug record, drinking problem, zero gang affiliations and no children. He had good credit, and he was in the military. We began to date months later; he did not rush me to do anything, and we got along very well. We stayed together and became even closer because of everything that I was going through with my mother.

Several months passed, and I began to hear my mother coughing during the night; she had been coughing a lot. It seemed to be getting worst, to the point I could not take it anymore, so I called 911. I did not know at the time, but this was the last time I would see her. She passed away in the hospital of congested heart failure. I did not get a chance to see her before she left this earth.

After her passing, my sister's boyfriend wanted to sing at her funeral, and I was not having that. He always thought he could do whatever he wanted, and I was not going to let him make a mockery of my mother's funeral.

POEM

Some folk did not treat us right,
not fair at all.

When the times were good, it was a
different story, until her fall.

Yes, trouble had a hold of her,

That much was so true.

I know she did her best even when she
was blue.

Feelings of being down and out,

Became the new normal for her.

It was so painful,
which sometimes would cause her
to go on a bender.

9

REMEMBERING
LIVING ON THE CUSP

So, I would visit Sharon, my special needs sister, on the weekends. This time would be different. I spoke to my sister, and she told me that she had my back. Thankfully, I was welcome to come back to her place if I wanted to. This time I was pregnant. She also told me that I could do whatever I wanted as far as the baby was concerned, so I moved back to the projects again. However, I moved constantly between my sister's house, Lawrence's house.

Lawrence kept his word, and we moved into a house with his sister, which was short-lived. Lawrence worked two jobs simultaneously,

Wendy's and Taco Bell, so my pregnancy cravings were pretty much satisfied between the two restaurants. One day, I was warming up some food and left the oven door open. It melted two of the knobs on the stove. His sister started going off on me. I didn't understand the problem because I had done this many times when I lived with my sister, and no knobs ever melted because of it. It got so bad living there that I decided to move back in with my sister because I wanted to be free of the stress. Yet he stayed there without me for a short while.

After the birth of our first child, we were still struggling, broke with not much education. I kept our vision of having our own home built from the ground, even though people doubted us. I was still mourning my mother on top of everything else that was going on. It was just crazy for me with little support, and we had challenges. We decided to let everything in the past stay there. I explained my life decisions to him and he accepted them. We decided to make it work no matter what came our way. After moving back together, we knew that we had to make it, not just for us, but for our own family.

After our second child, we moved into a studio apartment while working very hard to reach our goals. Being parents together was somewhat hard for us because he was really strict. He liked things to be in order, but he was a tad over the top, his actions were offensive toward some of my friends, and family was not exempt. By the time I turned twenty-one, I was ready to do something different, and my so-called friends did not make it any better. They were always out having fun, and I wanted to have fun too! I really never had any company because Lawrence never wanted me to have anyone over.

I was confused somewhat because I did not want to feel stuck. Many families got caught-up in the projects for generations, and we did not want that for our children or us. We both worked hard during this time and reported all income to the landlord, even though it caused our rent to increase. Before my birthday, we began to fall apart. I wanted something different; I wanted to go out to the club.

I started clubbing because I wanted something different, but I could not figure out what I was longing for in life. Some of my friends would tell me things like, "Girl, you need to at least date around before you get married. You can do better."

Nevertheless, I chose to give power to those words and asked for a separation. He really did not want this because he wanted to keep our family together. Even after the proposal, I wanted out, just for a little while. We had a wonderful, loving babysitter who lived across the street. I thought, *how much better can it get than this?* She was my son's godmother, and I knew she would take good care of both children. So, I started going out and meeting new people.

Lawrence and I had an understanding that our mission was for the short-term. After a while, he offered to stick it out and let my phase pass, but I felt that it would not be fair or right to either one of us. I felt like it was time to leave, so I did.

Ronald

I met this guy named **Ronald,** and I said to myself, *He is the one*. He was a short guy in the Navy with a great big smile. We made each other look great, and things went smoothly; that is, until I met this other guy, Ray.

We went through some drama, but it all came to a head one evening when my boyfriend Ronald came to my house, and Ray was sleeping in the living room with my friends and family. My man Ronald demanded that I wake him up and tell him to leave. I refused because he was just my friend, and he was so mad that he left, and relocated. He dumped me. I was in disbelief.

Months later, Ray captured my heart, and we were married six months later. It was a great thing for both of us because we were in love, and we wanted to walk this journey together. We got married, and he got stationed in Mobile, Alabama. We went from there to Pascagoula, Mississippi. We stayed in Mobile, which was interesting to say the least. I got pregnant with my youngest son after arriving in Pascagoula, Mississippi. It was very different than any place I had ever been to, but I tried to take it as a military wife. I stayed to myself, with the exception of a few military families, and it worked out overall.

One young lady wanted to sleep with my husband shortly after we separated, and she had her own husband, but that did not matter. When I confronted her, she told me that they just went to a movie, and I knew that she was lying to me. It took everything in me to not report her and my husband to the commander in the Navy. Yet moving on, we both decided to separate when my son was six months old, and I decided to move to Pensacola, Florida. We just grew apart.

After settling in Florida, it was very nice but, I longed for my husband; he was shipped out to several locations outside of the USA. I was alone with three children and my special needs sister. It was hard, but I had to hang in there, and somewhere deep inside, I knew it would be okay. Many nights I cried, not knowing what the future would bring, and I did not want to go back to where I came from. I had to figure this out somehow.

I know that I did not have any real support. I thought about going back to the projects, but then I told myself that would be going backward. I knew that I did not want that for my children or me. I also thought about Wisconsin, a place that held so many memories, but I had not lived there as an adult. Well, I finally decided to go to Seattle, where my sister Carol and her husband lived with my nephew because I knew they would help me with my special needs sister and my children. After several conversations, I decided to move there. My sister and her husband came to Florida that week, and they offered to take the kids with them. Of course, I said yes.

I made it to Seattle, Washington, that winter of December 1995. I was so excited to have some support finally. I really enjoyed having family around, even those who took advantage of me, but I was okay with that. Within a few months, things kind of fell apart. I was waiting and ready for that to happen.

I moved into my own place and was working while going to school full-time. At this time, nobody around me was doing this. I finally bought a car. The kids went to KinderCare, and I went to college at Eton institute.

Day after day, I always felt like I was missing out on what everyone else had been doing all day. At this time, I was living in Kent, Washington. They turned our apartments into a low-income living space, and I did not qualify. I moved, and to top it off, I had a warning to be evicted because of something they accused my nephew of doing. I thought that my husband and I would have gotten back together, but that never happened.

POEM

Family

Family is what family is, this much is true,

Through the good and the bad…

Some you look forward to seeing,

They made your heart smile,

While others, you try to avoid due to the fact they make you sad.

You desire that one-day things will change,

Everyone on the same page, lifting each other up.

Truthfully, some are on the border of being deranged.

All you can do is accept each one for themselves,

To one degree or another.

You had no choice of who would be.

Your sister or brother.

*Embrace them with love, even if not,
return back to you,*

*One day you will understand it was
them just being true.*

*Not everything can be understood,
so move on through life.*

*People will sometime try to bring
strife upon you.*

10

THE STRUGGLE IS REAL

O ne day I went to the barbershop and was asked by the barber to visit his church; his pastor was in the shop as well. I agreed to visit, and it was one of the best decisions I ever made. After going to the church, I became a member. The Secretary of the church was an amazing woman. I would go by the office, and she was so positive as well as supportive of me. She would even give me scriptures to read. I began to heal, so I continued to keep going along with my family.

In the next few years, I lost more family, but I stayed in church and served in the outreach ministry and later as an usher. I really felt the love from my church family; it was amazing to be a part of something like this during this time. I spent a lot of time reading God's word, and I joined the choir even though I could not sing, but I was a true worshiper.

Years passed, and I was getting ready for my firstborn to graduate from high school, and that was very exciting for me. My baby was now a young lady, and I was proud of her and myself.

One evening my best friend asked me to go and listen to some live music. I agreed, so I got all dolled up since I had not been out for a while. Then she canceled, but I went anyway. I met this guy, older than I, who had a strong southern accent. He was a nice-looking too. I went out again the next evening, and he gave me his business card. We talked on the phone for hours, and he had such a great sense of humor my jaws would get tired from laughing so hard. We really had a connection even though he lived in Tennessee; it was not long before he asked me to be his woman.

I explained to him how important church was for me, and he said that he understood where I was coming from. Once we started dating, he would fly back and forth to see me and send for me to see him. It did not take long before he proposed to me on Valentine's Day, and I accepted. He totally understood when it came to my sister, and that was very important to me. I knew one day my children would grow up and start their own lives, but my sister would still be with me. I needed someone who would accept my special needs sister as they accepted me. It didn't work out, to make a long story short, I called the wedding off and we remain friends to this day.

I had to start over again. I started a ministry called ISI, which meant Iron Sharpens Iron based on the scripture Proverbs 27:17. It was a ministry for Christian singles. I realized that most churches would focus on married couples, so I wanted an option for singles like myself – a place where it all about us coming together to grow and learn from each other. I rented a place for the first three Fridays of the month for a few hours, I supplied food, refreshments, Christian comedians, praise dancers and had guest speakers.

During this time, I worked a full-time job, so right after work on those days, I would run errands for the gathering and then go home to fulfill my duties. This went on for a while until one day I woke up and I was sick. I went to the ER, and they told me that I had a bleeding ulcer. They put me a special diet, so many things were on the list that I was advised to avoid.

The next time at church, we had a guest speaker, and I felt like he was talking to me, and then I realized that God did not want me to be sick. I had to learn how to delegate – period! So, I decided to bless the church with my ministry. This was a time for healing, forgiving, and loving myself. I just needed some *me* time.

Years later, I was getting ready for my youngest child to graduate, and I would be an empty-nester. Even though I was happy, it was also bittersweet because I did not want him to move out of the state even though I would still have my sister, and we would be together. Still, tragedy struck again with the passing of another family member. This time it was my nephew who had been in my corner, and now he had been murdered. I had to keep it together for myself and my family, it was a senseless tragedy. We had to be there for each other, and it was very hard on all of us, especially going back and forth to court. We wanted justice and closure more than anything because I just kept thinking about what my mother had went through with my sister's death, which had such an impact on my life and many family members.

The very next year, I lost another nephew to gun violence also, and it was another blow. It has been tough to get through the loss of my young nephews, and the fact that they both left behind children was even more heartbreaking. Through the hardships, I never let go of Jesus no matter how hard it became for me. One may look at me from the outside and say what they want, but I thank God he looks at my heart. I never claim to be a perfect person, but I love the only perfect One who died for a sinner like me. I have always felt the presence of God throughout my whole life.

As a young child, I recall asking Him to grant me just one more thing, and I would not ask for anything else. But I would ask again and again, and He always answered every time. He would do it for and me. At the end of the day, no matter how hard times have been and the many hardships throughout my life, I always knew that it could be worst without Jesus as my silver lining. With that, I have chosen to continue to keep my faith, praise, and worship Him through the good and the bad times. Knowing that He promised never to leave or forsake me, I will just continue to work on myself as He works in me. So, my advice to anyone reading this book is that no matter what comes your way, you can get through it, so keep the faith in the midst of your storms. God has all the power and unlimited love for us all. I genuinely believe that I would not be where I am if not for the love of God in my life. Many things hurt, confused me, and made me feel as if I was forgotten. The challenges made me feel lost and alone. I felt like no one understood or experienced the things I had been through, making me think that I was the only one. Looking back, Jesus was there with me, as the poem *Footprints in the Sand* offered to us all. I only saw my own footsteps because he was carrying me the whole time. I could have been dead, in prison, a drug addict, a bad mom, or not been in a position to care for my special needs sister for over thirty-three years. So, I am sharing my testimony, and I hope that it encourages you to hang on no matter what life sends your way. Please know that Jesus loves you. He carries you through it all.

POEM

Sanity

Holding on to sanity is a task to be tackled,

It can destroy what you built.

Some struggle but know that you are not alone on this journey,

Many have issues that affected them due to no fault of their own,

Somehow you now have to find a way out to escape,

Then some realize that finding a way to let go,

Trust Christ, then new life begins.

Old things have to be put to rest, trust him only,

Then you can begin to heal from wounds old and new.

The Struggle is Real

POEM

The Porch

Heaven is my goal- are words that touch me deep inside,

I know that I fall short more often then I want to,
Learning how to be teachable is vital to living a better life.

Life can really be a humbling experience so learn along the way,
To continue to repeat life's' lessons equals a make-up test.

Made in the USA
Coppell, TX
27 November 2020

42264340R00049